To the Extreme

Skydiving

by Mandy R. Marx

Reading Consultant:
Barbara J. Fox
Reading Specialist
North Carolina State University

Capstone
press

Mankato, Minnesota

Blazers is published by Capstone Press,
151 Good Counsel Drive, P.O. Box 669, Mankato, Minnesota 56002.
www.capstonepress.com

Library of Congress Cataloging-in-Publication Data
Marx, Mandy R.
　　Skydiving / by Mandy R. Marx.
　　p. cm.—(Blazers. To the extreme)
　　Includes bibliographical references and index.
　　ISBN-13: 978-0-7368-5464-1 (hardcover)
　　ISBN-10: 0-7368-5464-9 (hardcover)
　　1. Skydiving—Juvenile literature. I. Title. II. Series.
GV770.M37 2006
791.5'6—dc22　　　　　　　　　　　　　　　　2005019603

Summary: Describes the sport of skydiving, including equipment,
　　competitions, and safety information.

Editorial Credits
Carrie A. Braulick, editor; Jason Knudson, set designer; Kate Opseth
　　and Jennifer Bergstrom, book designers; Wanda Winch, photo
　　researcher; Scott Thoms, photo editor

Photo Credits
Aboveallphotography/Jason Peters, 6, 7, 26
Corbis/Reuters/Sukree Sukplang, 5
Getty Images Inc./Stone/Joe McBride, 14; Taxi/Brian Erler, cover
Joel Kiesel, 15, 22, 28–29
Photo courtesy Chris Reeves, 11, 12, 21
Photo Network Stock/Daniel J. McCleery, 18–19
Photophile LLC, 13
Photri/T. Sanders, 17
Red Bull Photofiles/Rick Neves, 8
Skydiving Stunts/Greg Gasson, 25

The author dedicates this book to Dan, with whom she took the
ultimate plunge.

1 2 3 4 5 6 11 10 09 08 07 06

Table of Contents

Out of the Blue

An airplane soars above the clouds. One by one, skydivers leap out. They fall at speeds of at least 100 miles (161 kilometers) per hour.

The skydivers twist, tumble, and turn. They grab onto one another to make patterns in the sky.

After a minute of free-falling, the skydivers drift apart. They open their parachutes and glide gracefully to the ground.

BLAZER FACT

Chinese drawings that are at least 1,000 years old show people using parachutes.

Gearing Up

Skydivers love the excitement of their dangerous sport. Proper use of their gear is all that separates them from certain death.

Skydivers strap parachute packs
to their backs. They pop open the
parachute canopy to land safely.

Canopy

13

BLAZER FACT

Skydivers open parachutes between 2,500 and 3,500 feet (760 and 1,000 meters) above the ground.

Altimeter

Skydivers must open their parachutes at the right altitude, or height above the ground. Altimeters show skydivers how high they are.

No skydiver wants to land in the
middle of nowhere! Skydivers use
steering toggles to turn. Then they can
land in a safe place.

Skydiving Diagram

Lines

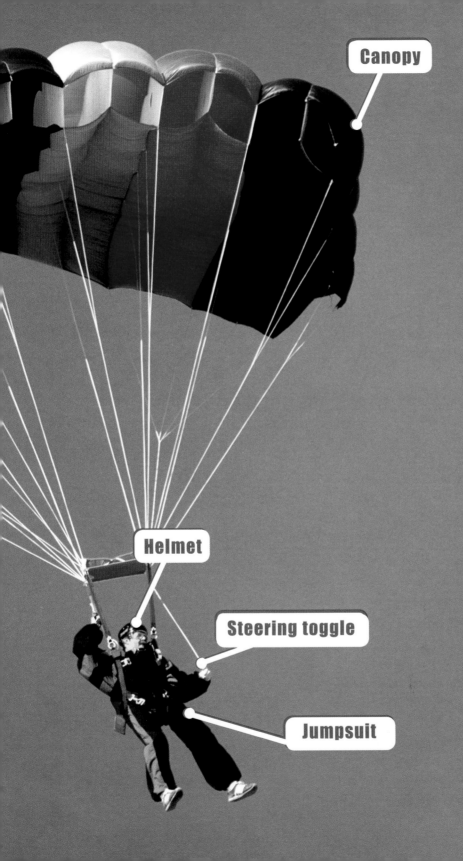

Canopy

Helmet

Steering toggle

Jumpsuit

Safe Skydiving

Skydivers train on the ground before they set foot in a plane. They learn how to make safe jumps and handle emergencies.

Skydivers depend on their main parachute to work. But if it doesn't, they open a reserve parachute.

BLAZER FACT

Some reserve parachutes open on their own if the skydiver never opens the main parachute.

Competitions

Skydivers compete in two main types of events. In freestyle competitions, they do gymnastics in the air.

In relative work competitions, skydivers join together to create detailed patterns. They hope their patterns will win them first place.

BLAZER FACT

In June 2004, 372 people set the world record for the largest relative work formation.

A thrilling raft ride in the sky!

Glossary

altimeter (al-TIM-uh-tur)—an instrument that shows the altitude of an object

free fall (FREE FAWL)—the part of a skydiver's jump before the parachute opens

freestyle (FREE-stile)—a type of skydiving in which skydivers perform gymnastic moves

gymnastics (jim-NASS-tiks)—difficult and carefully controlled body movements

parachute (PA-ruh-shoot)—a large piece of strong, lightweight fabric; parachutes allow people to jump from high places and float safely to the ground.

relative work (REL-uh-tiv WURK)—a type of skydiving in which skydivers work together to form patterns in the sky

Read More

Cefrey, Holly. *Skysurfing.* X-treme Outdoors. New York: Children's Press, 2003.

Hopkins, Ellen. *Air Devils: Sky Racers, Sky Divers, and Stunt Pilots.* Cover-to-Cover Books. Logan, Iowa: Perfection Learning, 2000.

Schindler, John E. *Skydiving.* Extreme Sports. Milwaukee: Gareth Stevens, 2005.

Internet Sites

FactHound offers a safe, fun way to find Internet sites related to this book. All of the sites on FactHound have been researched by our staff.

Here's how:

1. Visit *www.facthound.com*
2. Type in this special code **0736854649** for age-appropriate sites. Or enter a search word related to this book for a more general search.
3. Click on the **Fetch It** button.

FactHound will fetch the best sites for you!

Index